GIVE *ideals* THIS CHRISTMAS . . . Let *ideals* express your heartfelt wishes at every season of the year!

WE'LL SEND A GIFT ANNOUNCEMENT WITH THE FIRST ISSUE!

Every issue of *Ideals* is bursting with a celebration of life's special times: Christmas, Thanksgiving, Easter, Mother's Day, Country and Friendship. Give a gift subscription to *Ideals* this Christmas and you will bring joy to the lives of special people six times a year! Each issue offers page after page of magnificent photographs, exquisite drawings and paintings, delightful stories and poetry. Each is a "keeper" that invites the reader back, again and again, to look, read and ponder. There's nothing quite as special as a gift of *Ideals*!

SAVE 44%
off the bookstore price!
To order, mail card below

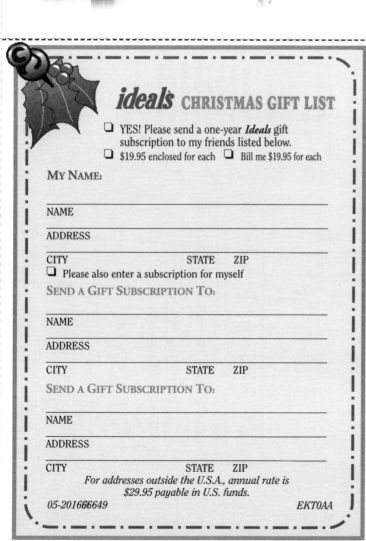

ideals CHRISTMAS GIFT LIST

❏ YES! Please send a one-year *Ideals* gift subscription to my friends listed below.
❏ $19.95 enclosed for each   ❏ Bill me $19.95 for each

MY NAME:

NAME

ADDRESS

CITY   STATE   ZIP
❏ Please also enter a subscription for myself

SEND A GIFT SUBSCRIPTION TO:

NAME

ADDRESS

CITY   STATE   ZIP

SEND A GIFT SUBSCRIPTION TO:

NAME

ADDRESS

CITY   STATE   ZIP

For addresses outside the U.S.A., annual rate is $29.95 payable in U.S. funds.

05-201666649   EKT0AA

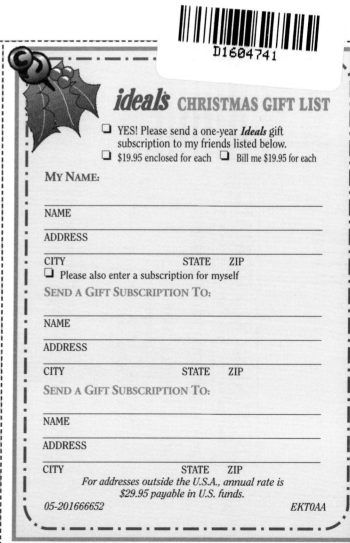

ideals CHRISTMAS GIFT LIST

❏ YES! Please send a one-year *Ideals* gift subscription to my friends listed below.
❏ $19.95 enclosed for each   ❏ Bill me $19.95 for each

MY NAME:

NAME

ADDRESS

CITY   STATE   ZIP
❏ Please also enter a subscription for myself

SEND A GIFT SUBSCRIPTION TO:

NAME

ADDRESS

CITY   STATE   ZIP

SEND A GIFT SUBSCRIPTION TO:

NAME

ADDRESS

CITY   STATE   ZIP

For addresses outside the U.S.A., annual rate is $29.95 payable in U.S. funds.

05-201666652   EKT0AA

Do your Christmas shopping today and SAVE 44%

off the regular bookstore price of *Ideals* when you give a one-year subscription!

ONLY $19⁹⁵

Everyone knows at least two or three people who would love a gift subscription to *Ideals*! It's a very special Christmas gift that keeps on reminding a close friend or relative of your thoughtfulness all through the year. And, when you order now, you enjoy a generous savings off the regular bookstore price—and do your Christmas shopping right away!

for each one-year gift subscription of six issues— a savings of $15.75 off the bookstore price.

To order today, use one or both of the postage-paid reply cards (see reverse side).

Add more gifts, if you wish, by enclosing a separate list with the additional names and addresses and mailing in an envelope to:

Ideals Publications, Inc.
A Division of Guideposts
P.O. Box 576
Brewster NY 10509-0576

SEND NO MONEY NOW—WE'LL BILL YOU LATER!

Orders received after December 1 will start with the Easter issue.

ideals®
THANKSGIVING

More Than 50 Years of Celebrating Life's Most Treasured Moments

Vol. 58, No. 5

Thou crownest the year with Thy goodness.

—*Psalm 65:11*

Featured Photograph
6

A Slice of Life
8

Bits and Pieces
12

From My
Garden Journal
16

For the Children
22

Devotions from
the Heart
33

Readers' Reflections
36

Handmade Heirloom
44

Legendary Americans
48

Traveler's Diary
50

Collector's Corner
58

Ideals' Family Recipes
62

Through My
Window
64

Remember When
76

Country Chronicle
80

Readers' Forum
86

IDEALS—Vol. 58, No. 5 September MMI IDEALS (ISSN 0019-137X, USPS 256-240)
is published six times a year: January, March, May, July, September, and November by
IDEALS PUBLICATIONS, a division of Guideposts.
39 Seminary Hill Road, Carmel, NY 10512.
Copyright © MMI by IDEALS PUBLICATIONS, a division of Guideposts.
All rights reserved. The cover and entire contents of IDEALS are fully protected by copyright
and must not be reproduced in any manner whatsoever.
Title IDEALS registered U.S. Patent Office. Printed and bound in USA by Quebecor Printing.

Printed on Weyerhaeuser Husky. The paper used in this publication meets the minimum requirements of
American National Standard for Information Sciences—
Permanence of Paper for Printed Library Materials, ANSI Z39.48-1984.

Periodicals postage paid at Carmel, New York, and additional mailing offices.
POSTMASTER: Send address changes to Ideals, 39 Seminary Hill Road, Carmel, NY 10512.
For subscription or customer service questions, contact Ideals Publications,
a division of Guideposts, 39 Seminary Hill Road, Carmel, NY 10512. Fax 845-228-2115.

Reader Preference Service: We occasionally make our mailing lists available to
other companies whose products or services might interest you.
If you prefer not to be included, please write to Ideals Customer Service.

ISBN 0-8249-1169-5 GST 893989236

Visit *Ideals*'s website at www.idealspublications.com

Cover Photo: Sugar maple in Pennsylvania. Photo by Fred Habegger/Grant Heilman Photography, Inc.
Artwork this page: Calla lilies. Stacy Venturi Pickett, Artist.
Inside Front Cover: CLEARING OFF—AUTUMN ON THE DELAWARE. *Thomas Worthington Whittredge, Artist. Christie's Images.*
Inside Back Cover: CONVERSATION AT THE FENCE. *Jasper Francis Cropsey, Artist. Christie's Images.*

AUTUMN GLORY

Gladys Harp

I am rich today with autumn's gold,
All that my covetous hands can hold:
Frost-painted leaves and goldenrod,
A goldfinch on a milkweed pod,
Huge golden pumpkins in the field
With heaps of corn from a bounteous yield,
Golden apples heavy on the trees
Rivaling those of Hesperides,
Golden rays of balmy sunshine spread
Over all like butter on warm bread;
And the harvest moon will this night unfold
The streams running full of molten gold.
Oh, who could find a dearth of bliss
With autumn glory such as this?

AUTUMN PAGEANTRY

Neva Carlson

The ancient earth is spending summer's lore
And turns again to dreaming in the sun.
The orchard is yielding up its rubied store
Of McIntosh and crisp, ripe Jonathan.
The maple is blushing crimson on the hill;
The sumac shares its red and amber flame.
A silver birch outbids, with modest skill,
The bravest star that hangs in autumn's frame.
September is lavish with her Midas hand,
And shock and sheaf return a thousandfold;
And left upon the dreaming stubble land
Is autumn's footprint, etched in harvest gold.

Fall foliage scatters along a walkway in Portland, Oregon.
Photo by Steve Terrill.

Harvest

Isla Paschal Richardson

Enough that as the calendar is spent
There are a few that we call perfect days.
One crisp October day whose hazy sun
Streams warm and golden on the tapestry
Of autumn woods; or some bright day in March
When daffodils and furry pearl-gray tufts
Of pussy willow buds proclaim the spring
And promise all the mysteries of May;
Or one cool, silver, perfumed night in June
With stars rekindling age-old wonderings;
A sparkling morning in December when
You wake to find each tree and shrub arrayed
In glistening ermine and each field a vast,
Inviting, untrod carpet, dazzling white.
Though in between are rain and wind and storms,
Or dull, drab, cloudy hours, it is enough
That sprinkled through the year some perfect days
Sink deep into our being, and these few
We gather as our harvest to reclaim.

*Left: Native prairie grasses provide a backdrop for an aged wagon
and fence in Bureau County, Illinois. Photo by Terry Donnelly.
Overleaf: Fall comes to Buckeye Creek Lake in North Carolina's
Blue Ridge Mountains. Photo by Norman Poole.*

A SLICE OF LIFE

Edgar A. Guest

Art by Eve DeGrie

OCTOBER

Days are gettin' shorter and the air a keener snap;
Apples now are droppin' into Mother Nature's lap.
The mist at dusk is risin' over valley, marsh, and fen;
And it's just as plain as sunshine winter's comin' on again.

The turkeys now are struttin' round the old farmhouse once more;
They are done with all their nestin' and their hatchin' days are o'er.
Now the farmer's cuttin' fodder for the silo towerin' high,
And he's frettin' and complainin' cause the corn's a bit too dry.

But the air is mighty peaceful and the scene is good to see,
And there's somethin' in October that stirs deep inside of me.
And I can't help in believin' in a God above us when
Everything is ripe for harvest and the frost is back again.

Edgar A. Guest began his illustrious career in 1895 at the age of fourteen, when his work first appeared in the Detroit Free Press. *His column was syndicated in more than three hundred newspapers, and he became known as "The Poet of the People."*

On an October Hill

Katherine Berle Stains

While Bob may bring an axe to steal the gold,
His Ann will have the bread for dining there,
And Meg will carry all her bag will hold
Of brushes, paints to capture colors rare.
And brother Don will kick the leaves around
While puppies bark and circle in their play,
But I will walk for miles without a sound
To see how God has made an autumn day.

To have, to fill, to do will often seem
An answer giving me a thing desired,
But when a day will come and troubles team
And strike me flat and make me wretched, tired,
I'll dig and sort through packaged days until
I find October on a distant hill.

The October day is a dream,
bright and beautiful as the rainbow,
and as brief and fugitive.

—W. Hamilton Gibson

Young bike riders enjoy a crisp October day in
New Hampshire's White Mountains National Forest.
Photo by Londie G. Padelsky.

BITS & PIECES

Once more the liberal year laughs out
O'er richer stores than gems or gold;
Once more with harvest song and shout
Is nature's boldest triumph told.
—*John Greenleaf Whittier*

Earth is here so kind, that just tickle
her with a hoe and she laughs
with a harvest.
—*Douglas Jerrold*

Fear not that I shall mar so fair a harvest
by putting in my sickle ere 'tis ripe.
—*John Home*

Autumn into earth's lap does throw
Brown apples gay in a game of play.
—*Dinah Mulock Craik*

He that hath a good harvest
may be content with some thistles.
—*English proverb*

*I*n harvesttime, harvest-folk, servants and all
Should make altogether good cheer in the fall.
—*Thomas Tusser*

*T*hy bounty shines in autumn unconfined
And spreads a common feast for all that live.
—*James Thomson*

*S*ome have meat and cannot eat,
And some would eat that want it;
But we have meat, and we can eat,
And so the Lord be thanked.
—*Robert Burns*

Autumn Morning

Joan McCall Taylor

Gray and misty is the dawn,
And then a glint of gold
Appears above the purple ridge,
Its magic to behold.
A streak of crimson lights the sky;
The grayness turns to blue.
The earth is painted by the brush
Of early morning dew.

GRAY

Esther Wood

All the things that wait are gray:
The mist that tucks the sun away,
The quiet dew that feeds the earth,
A seed before its lovely birth,
The clouds that color autumn skies,
The heads of those grown old and wise,
A tree that's silvery with spring,
A nest of sparrows born to sing,
A budding branch, a dawning day—
All the things that wait are gray.

*A gray haze falls over a pear orchard in Hood
River County, Oregon. Photo by Steve Terrill.*

From My Garden Journal

Lisa Ragan

PAMPAS GRASS

As we approach late autumn and the weather turns cooler, I delight in a slow walk through my garden with a mug of warm, mulled cider. I take a sort of inventory while I walk and notice what chores await me—leaves to rake, plants to cut back for their winter sleep, and the last of the annuals to remove. Then I come to the star of my winter garden—the pampas grass. With its beautiful, once-white plumes waving gracefully to the sky, my lone specimen of pampas grass still shines in full glory. The feathery plumes have softened to the color of café au lait, but the full skirt of foliage remains green.

Pampas grass is perhaps the most popular of all ornamental grasses grown in the United States. Our fascination with ornamental grasses soared during the Victorian era when pampas grass became a decorating sensation. Amidst the fringed lamps, needlepoint footstools, and lace curtains of Victorian parlors would be the glorious plumage of pampas grass bursting from an urn. The plant itself enjoyed center stage in stylish, turn-of-the-century gardens. By the 1920s, pampas grass fell from popularity, but the passion surged again among many suburban homeowners of the 1940s, who planted a specimen or two of pampas grass in their front lawns. The popularity of this majestic perennial continues today.

Native to South America, pampas grass is an exotic, ornamental grass that grows quite differently in its native habitat than in suburbia. This graceful giant spreads across the grassy plains, or *pampas*, of Argentina, Brazil, and Chile.

The plumes of pampas grass tower up to ten feet high, and its large mound of evergreen foliage spreads from six to eight feet. Ranging in color from green to gray-green, the leaves of the plant are sword shaped and serrated with razor-like edges that can lacerate any bare-armed gardener. Early Spanish settlers in South America named pampas grass *cortadera*, meaning "the cutter." The "flowers" of ornamental grasses are called *inflorescences:* long, slender spikes of tiny, delicate flower clusters which give the plumes of pampas grass their feathery appearance. They have a silky look when first sprouting and become fluffier as they mature. The inflorescences of pampas grass are unusual in that they are entirely female on one plant and entirely male on another plant. If plants of both sexes are planted together, little seedlings may appear. Propagation is best achieved, however, by dividing the plant in the spring. Female plants are generally prized above male specimens for their larger, hardier plumes.

A wide selection of cultivated varieties of

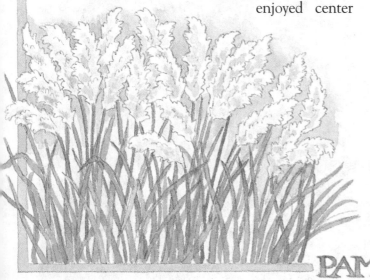

pampas grass exists today, with ranges of plume color, leaf color, and height. Most of the named cultivars are female plants. White-plumed pampas grasses include Silver Comet, Silver Beacon, Silver Fountain, Sunningdale Silver, and Silver Stripe (Albolineata). For a warm-toned, more golden appearance, gardeners can select Aureolineata, Gold Band, which grows to a manageable five-and-a-half-feet high and features leaves tipped in a gold color that deepens as the fall season nears its end. A popular cultivar with suburban gardeners, Pumila is also called dwarf pampas grass due to its "short" stature of six feet in height. Pumila is especially popular not only for its compact size but also for its plentiful feathery plumes. For pastel shades of plumes, consider the large-sized variety Rendatleri, also called pink pampas grass for its rose-colored inflorescences. Carnea is a cultivar that has shorter stems than Rendatleri and features pink plumes in a slightly paler shade. For a striking purple color, the cultivar Violacea offers plumes flushed with a lovely purple hue.

If planted in a suitably mild climate, pampas grass should remain healthy for many years. The plant will reach its optimum height and girth if planted in a sunny location with sufficient moisture. Although it can grow in lesser conditions, the plant will not reach peak form. Pampas grass will live in a variety of soil types but prefers fertile, well-drained soil. Remarkably heat-tolerant, pampas grass can stand out as a feature in desert gardens and can be sensitive to cold weather. When selecting the best spot in your garden for pampas grass, consider placing it against a backdrop of darker foliage, such as a stand of pine, where the white plumes will stand out. Pampas grass can also accent any small stand of water, such as a pond or slow stream, and the reflection of this massive beauty in the water can be stunning. Light is also an important consideration when choosing the ideal location for pampas grass. Although it needs strong sun, some garden-

ers choose to place pampas grass in a spot where it can be backlit by the descending sun, which will cause the plant to glow. This graceful ornamental grass can be planted as a group in large, open spaces to provide a natural wind break.

Pampas grass will usually thrive with either light or no feedings. When planting your specimen, you may choose to include some organic manure in the hole and also use it as an annual mulching. Be sure to wear sturdy, leather gloves to protect yourself from the cutting edges of the leaves. Pampas grass will need healthy waterings in order to establish it properly in your garden.

Gardeners who harvest the plumes for drying should cut them just before they have completely opened. While the inflorescences are drying, they will continue to open to their fullest form, and cutting them early will help to prevent unnecessary disintegration of the dried plume. Pampas grass is rarely troubled by any disease, although some specimens have been known to fall prey to rust, a fungus which produces rust-colored spots on the leaves. Rust prevention includes good garden maintenance such as regularly removing dead leaves from around the plant and ensuring it gets enough air circulation.

Aphids and mealy bugs will dine happily upon pampas grass if given ample opportunity. Aphids can usually be removed successfully with soapy water or insecticidal soap, and mealy bugs can be destroyed by swabbing the plant with alcohol.

As for my own garden, I regret that I cannot plant a stately row of pampas grass as an oversized wind break and enjoy it much as it grows on the grasslands of Argentina. My limited city lot does, however, provide room enough for my treasured single specimen—an elegant tribute to a South American treasure.

Lisa Ragan tends her small but mighty city garden in Nashville, Tennessee, with the help of her two shih-tzu puppies, Clover and Curry.

The Constancy of Seasons

May Smith White

Each fading bloom today is autumn-wise.
A deep conspiracy is close at hand
As leaves all move like some great rhythmic band,
And from the distance come the wild-geese cries.

Each season seems a mystery that lies
As if deep-buried in the quiet land;
And many times in awe we mutely stand
Because it always leaves some broken ties.

We grow complacent in these present times
And fail to plan for days that lie ahead
Like nature plans for changes sure to come
As suddenly as do a poet's rhymes.
We must be like the seasons, hold no dread,
But harvest now each final autumn crumb.

Autumn

Myrtle Leora Nelson

When summer flowers are gone and autumn embers
Burst forth in splendor with a golden glow,
Oh, I am happy in the joy of living
When pensive autumn makes her gorgeous bow.

The air is crisp; the maple leaves are yellow;
Their trunks are storing sugar sweet and good.
The squirrels and other tiny woodland creatures
Have found a place to hoard their winter's food.

The trees are dropping apples in the orchard;
The moon's a golden lantern up above.
And everywhere we look we see reflected
The goodness of our gracious God of love.

A room gathers the year's final blossoms. Photo by Jessie Walker.

SCARLET MAPLES

Agnes Davenport Bond

In autumn's chilly days, the maple trees
Have changed their robes of green to scarlet hue.
Their high tops quiver with each stirring breeze,
Which adds more color from a distant view.
But while the trees are gay in harvest days,
Their falling leaves remind the passersby
That branches soon will lose their fall bouquets,
And naked limbs will stretch across the sky.

Yet while the ground is covered with this spread
Of nature's forest carpet, soft and cool,
The village children jump about and tread
Within its confines on their way from school.
These treasured hours spent in childhood glee
Are oft recalled in later years they see.

LEAVES

Elsie N. Brady

How silently they tumble down
And come to rest upon the ground
To lay a carpet, rich and rare,
Beneath the trees without a care,
Content to sleep, their work well done,
Colors gleaming in the sun.

At other times, they wildly fly
Until they nearly reach the sky.
Twisting, turning through the air
Till all the trees stand stark and bare.
Exhausted, drop to earth below
To wait, like children, for the snow.

*Right: Children enjoy autumn's treasures. Photo by
Mitch Diamond/International Stock.
Border: A carpet of maple leaves. Photo by Superstock.*

FOR THE CHILDREN

Familiar Friends

James S. Tippett

The horses, the pigs,
And the chickens,
The turkeys, the ducks,
And the sheep!
I can see all my friends
From my window
As soon as I waken
From sleep.

The cat on the fence
Is out walking.
The geese have gone down
For a swim.
The pony comes trotting
Right up to the gate;
He knows I have candy
For him.

The cows in the pasture
Are switching
Their tails to keep off
The flies.
And the old mother dog
Has come out in the yard
With five pups to give me
A surprise.

COME JOIN US
FOR A HAYRIDE

Nita Cain

The wagon waiting by the barn
Is filled with new-mown hay,
So come and join us for a ride
At eventide today.

The harvest moon will lead us
Down the shadowed winding lane;
And as we cuddle close, we'll sing
An oldentime refrain.

The chilly breeze at dusk will bring
The scent of ripened wheat.
What other scent has nature made
More delicately sweet?

Beyond the cornstalks piled high
Like wigwams, we will pass
And gather golden pumpkins from the
Frosty meadow grass.

Then dreaming solitary dreams
Of other autumns past
When we were young, we'll reminisce
And head back home at last.

There'll be cider, hot and steamy,
So please say that you will stay,
And come and join us for a ride
At eventide today.

*Selma and Emma, Percheron draft horses, pull a hayride to
the pumpkin patch at Peterson Apple Country in Oregon.
Photo by Steve Terrill.*

GOD AND AUTUMN

Levi H. Koehn

Let the brightness of this day
Tell of the brightness of Thy glory;
The warmth of the autumn sun
Of Thy enfolding love;
The blue that stretches out into the unknown
Of Thy boundless purity;
Let the wind speak of Thy spirit
Moving among men.

Let the rows of shocks in the field,
The bulging bins in the yards of our farms,
The well-fed cattle in the browning pasture
Speak of Thy goodness to men.

*A farmer finishes the evening chores on his Missouri farm.
Photo by Gay Bumgarner.*

Thanksgiving

Stella Craft Tremble

So many years have passed away
Since Pilgrims on Thanksgiving Day
At Plymouth met with fervent prayer
Their gratitude and food to share.
This is our land—the plains and hills,
The valleys where the sunshine spills
An amber light on beans and corn
Each time a golden day is born.
Today we think of pioneers
Who braved all dangers, met all fears,
Who planted in the fertile loam,
Who tamed frontiers to make a home.
For forest-store, for waterways,
For cotton fields, for mountain ore,
For mighty spires we sing our praise.
For scholars with intelligence
Who attained wisdom of the sage,
Who left their heritage to us
And flag of freedom to this age.
We thank Thee, God, for rain and sun,
For peace at frosty winter's edge,
For harvests and for vintage bells,
For faith and joy in work well done.
The flag we love now flies above;
May faith and virtue keep us strong
As we together sing this song:
"God bless Thanksgiving Day!"

An 1840s Thanksgiving prayer is reenacted at a living history farm in York County, South Carolina. Photo by Norman Poole.

Thanksgiving Prayer

Chris Ahlemann

I thank You, Lord, for harvest grain,
For plums and apples too,
For sunny days and gentle rain
And skies of deepest blue.

I thank You for a place called home
Where love and laughter live,
A place where all are safe and warm
And ready to forgive.

I thank You for the soothing peace
That comes at close of day
As I my fears and cares release
When I kneel down to pray.

Thankfulness

Kay Hoffman

We're thankful for Thy blessings, Lord,
Thy watchful eye above,
For freedom's bell that tolls for all
In this dear land we love.

We're thankful, Lord, for useful work,
For measure of good health,
For family ties and friendship dear,
More precious this than wealth.

For all Thy tender mercies, Lord,
For sunshine and for rain,
For golden harvest richly blessed
In yield of fruit and grain.

On this Thanksgiving Day, dear Lord,
We bow in humble prayer.
We're thankful for Thy blessings, Lord;
Thy gifts are everywhere.

*Rows of windows offer a unique view of the river
below. Photo by Mia Et Klaus/Superstock.*

Devotions FROM THE Heart

Pamela Kennedy

Enter into His gates with thanksgiving, and into His courts with praise: be thankful unto Him, and bless His name.
Psalm 100:4

THANKSGIVING IS THE KEY

Have you ever felt far from God? Sometimes it's as if we stand in a desert, emptiness stretching before us in every direction, wondering how we got here and longing to find a way home. When I ask thoughtful questions such as this, I have a practical and witty friend who often tosses out aphorisms.

"If you're feeling far from God," she told me once, "just look around and see who moved!" I understood what she meant, but her glib response wasn't very helpful. I may have moved away from God, but my present dilemma was to find a way back! I was in one of those places where trying harder just didn't seem to help. Then, leafing through my Bible one day, I stumbled upon a familiar psalm, the one-hundredth. I must have read it dozens of times before. I think I even memorized it as a child. But suddenly, one of the phrases seemed to jump off the page: *Enter into His gates with thanksgiving.* When I had read the psalm before, I always assumed this meant to be thankful whenever I approached a time of worship. But this time a small voice seemed to be whispering something quite different as I read the familiar words.

I pictured a great gate, closed and locked. There was no hope of climbing over it or of squeezing through the heavy bars. I was on the outside, looking in, shut out from the presence of God. And then I was handed a key. It fit the lock perfectly, and as I turned it, the gate swung open. I suddenly experienced the comforting knowledge that I was with my heavenly Father once more. I was safe, secure, home. What was the key? Thanksgiving! It was not only a way to behave, but also a way to unlock the entryway to the kingdom of heaven.

In giving thanks to God, we open the gates that separate us from His presence. These barriers might be walls of bitterness, barbed fences of anger, ramparts of resentment, or wide moats of despair and self-pity; those things that cause us to feel abandoned and lonely. But when we turn from our self-imposed barriers and instead acknowledge Him as the source of every good thing, gratitude spills into our hearts. The warming flood of thanksgiving pushes out the fear and hostility that isolate us.

Dear Father, help me to remember that a heart filled with thanksgiving is the key to experiencing the joy of Your loving presence.

I believe God wants us to have a clear and open access to His peace, joy, and contentment, but that we often wander off into other places—led away from God by worry, anxiety, and discontentment. At some point in our wanderings, we stop, look around, and realize we're far from God. We long to return home, but it's as if we're locked out. It is then that we can take up the key of thanksgiving, unlock the gates of heaven, and joyfully return to the place God wants us to be. He is not only waiting for us, eager for our homecoming, but He also freely offers us complete access to His kingdom.

This Thanksgiving, there is no reason for any of God's children to stay away from home. The welcome mat is out, the table is set, and the key has already been placed in our hands! Give thanks to the Lord for He is good, and His goodness extends to every generation.

A bamboo gate enters a garden in Seattle's Washington Park Arboretum. Photo by Terry Donnelly.

Autumn's Glory

May Smith White

This is the quiet day I long have sought
When burnished leaves hang mutely on each tree.
Here is true beauty, still untouched, unsought.
These scenes will live throughout eternity.
The autumn wind grows silent with her song
Like birds that cease their calls at end of day,
And one forgets that time was ever long
As yearning minds follow the last sunray.

True glory comes to every waiting heart,
As when the busy earth is brought to rest.
The fading rose adds to this timeless art
And waits the artist's brush to here attest.
Each autumn sings with joy still unsurpassed—
The present one more glorious than the last.

Autumn color spreads across Indiana's Hoosier Hills.
Photo by Daniel Dempster.

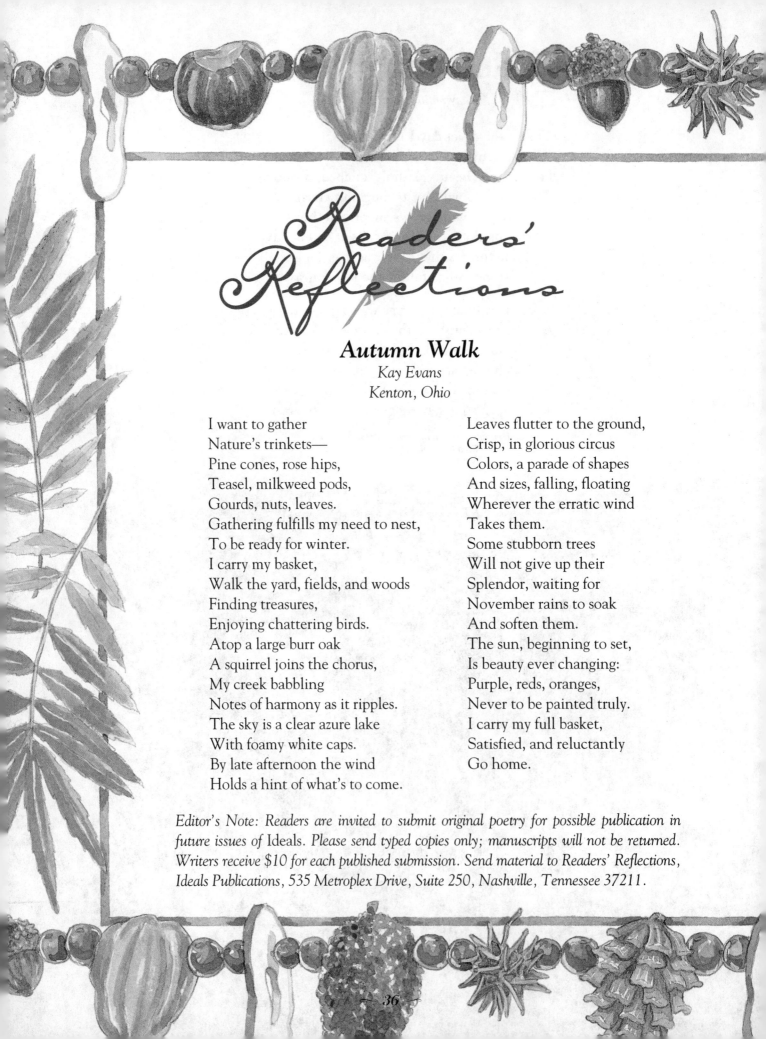

Readers' Reflections

Autumn Walk

Kay Evans
Kenton, Ohio

I want to gather
Nature's trinkets—
Pine cones, rose hips,
Teasel, milkweed pods,
Gourds, nuts, leaves.
Gathering fulfills my need to nest,
To be ready for winter.
I carry my basket,
Walk the yard, fields, and woods
Finding treasures,
Enjoying chattering birds.
Atop a large burr oak
A squirrel joins the chorus,
My creek babbling
Notes of harmony as it ripples.
The sky is a clear azure lake
With foamy white caps.
By late afternoon the wind
Holds a hint of what's to come.

Leaves flutter to the ground,
Crisp, in glorious circus
Colors, a parade of shapes
And sizes, falling, floating
Wherever the erratic wind
Takes them.
Some stubborn trees
Will not give up their
Splendor, waiting for
November rains to soak
And soften them.
The sun, beginning to set,
Is beauty ever changing:
Purple, reds, oranges,
Never to be painted truly.
I carry my full basket,
Satisfied, and reluctantly
Go home.

Editor's Note: Readers are invited to submit original poetry for possible publication in future issues of Ideals. Please send typed copies only; manuscripts will not be returned. Writers receive $10 for each published submission. Send material to Readers' Reflections, Ideals Publications, 535 Metroplex Drive, Suite 250, Nashville, Tennessee 37211.

Late Autumn Leaves

Carolyn Melbye
Roseville, Minnesota

Fallen, fallen to the brown earth below,
Rustling, crackling, wind-blown leaves,
Swirling and whirling to sheltered corners.
Dry leaves cozy together for escape
From winter snows and heavy-booted feet.
Leaves form a cover for field animals
And all of my fond summer memories.
Fallen, rustling, swirling late autumn leaves.

Autumn Souvenirs

Deborah Irvin
Gretna, Virginia

September flings her lukewarm days
To Indian summer's golden rays.
October sunset's purple hue
Regales a sky of denim blue.

Flaming leaves fly fancy free,
Dressing the earth in finery.
Wild geese flying V-formation
Hurry in anticipation.

The harvest moon's magic spell
Bathes frosty nights then bids farewell.
Soon snowy winter interferes
And covers up fall's souvenirs.

A New Season

Peggy Hill
Goff, Kansas

When the wheat is ripe,
We shall remember
To give thanks for bounty.

When the corn is reaching for the sky
And the milo heads are turning to rust,
We shall give praise for patience.

When the cows come up from the field,
We will recall how good it feels to go home.

And when the winter arrives and the
      ground is tired,
We shall remember to rest.

November

Louella V. Urbanczyk
Granite Bay, California

The winds have twirled the leaves all day;
From the trees the yellow leaves depart,
Skipping, dancing down the street
Like merry little hearts.

One last fling of autumn's moods,
The leaves and I together
Flaunt the endings of all things
And wink at winter weather.

Lines to Be Sent with a Gift of Hickory Nuts

Marion Doyle

A gift of little value in itself,
But with it comes a blue October day,
A flock of wild geese on their southward way;
A brief acquaintance with a garrulous elf,
A puckish robber with two bars of gold
Filched from the sun upon his russet back,
His wee elastic jaws a haversack
Filled with sweet shellbark provender: behold,
A chipmunk with the mumps!—A wise gourmet,
As you'll agree when from the pantry shelf
You take "just one more cookie," raptly savor
Its hickory crunchiness, and weakly waver,
"Well-l, just one more," escaping with your pelf,
Both hands well filled, your conscience neatly strung,
To loll before a glowing fire and weigh
All autumn's pungency upon your tongue.

Right: A chickaree enjoys a forest snack. Photo by Superstock.
Border: The forest floor gathers the trees' bounty in Missouri. Photo by Gay Bumgarner.

Woods Path
Mary Jeannette Bassett

Sun drenched, the russet needles lay
Close packed beneath my muffled feet.
Their fragrance filled the quiet wood,
And from the cedar where I stood
The cardinal's song was sweet.

Tall pines stretched upward toward the sky;
Persimmon trees were flecked with red
While flaming gums and scarlet oaks,
Wood maples in their yellow cloaks
Reached high above my head.

Where elderberry leaves had turned
And holly bushes crossed the trail,
The silver-coated squirrel played.
And through the autumn hush parade
The whirring wings of quail.

Autumn Climax
Johnielu Barber Bradford

I strolled the paths through nature's magic realm,
And half bare trees spread carpets for my feet.
I walked on nap from maple, oak, and elm
Where leaves of red and brown and yellow meet.
My path became a long and winding hall
Where spreading monarchs of the forest stood;
The stately trunks I passed, symmetrical and tall,
Were massive columns hued of living wood.
I dodged the falling leaves as they would drop
When high above some feathered songster moved,
And all about my feet lay summer's crop
Of ripened foliage in colors that I loved.

I marveled that from blight of frost and haze
Could come the climax of the autumn days.

Red pine trees rise through the autumn foliage in Michigan's
Hiawatha National Forest. Photo by Darryl Beers.

THANKSGIVING WINGS

Elisabeth Weaver Winstead

In autumn mists the pheasants fly
Across the cornfield's steepled sky.
The gypsy leaves come drifting down
In amber, rust, and burnished brown.

Ripe grapes flash jewels from each vine;
On hazy hills, persimmons shine;
The russet pears on laden trees
Are swaying in the wind-swept breeze.

Red apples with their scents to please
Are luring all the searching bees.
Fertile fields of hay are reaped;
In silos, fragrant feed lies heaped.

Chestnuts and walnuts carpet the ground;
Squirrels make raids on banquet found.
Gold-flecked yams, not far away,
Join pumpkin globes in bright display.

From fruitful earth is bounty spilled;
From glorious blessings, life's wonders filled.
To celebrate, we praise and sing
With hearts uplifted on Thanksgiving wings.

*A grateful thought toward
heaven is of itself a prayer.*

—GOTTHOLD EPHRAIM LESSING

Nature's goodness creates a colorful tabletop. Photo by Superstock.

◆ ◆ ◆

A trio of clocks offers a unique way to tell the time. Photo by Rick Lance. Stitched clock courtesy of Linda Butts.

CLOCK

Nancy Skarmeas

I love clocks and have at least one in every room of my house. My husband thinks I am overly obsessed with time, but I see it differently. I like the predictable routine of everyday life, and my clocks are the dependable anchors that guide me through that routine. Still, as much as I love crafts and clocks both, I always considered clockmaking the domain of expert artisans. Making my own clocks never even seemed within the realm of possibility. But what I didn't realize until recently is that there is clockmaking in the sense of building clock housing and assembling clockworks, which is definitely the work of master craftsmen, and then there is the making of clocks, which, with store-bought clockworks and a little creativity, is well within the reach of each and every one of us.

My mind was opened to the creative possibilities of clockmaking by an advertisement in a craft maga-zine for cross-stitched clock kits. I might have turned right past that page if not for the fact that one of the featured designs reminded me of a cross-stitch pattern familiar from my childhood. The ad featured several cross-stitched clock faces, one of which was a pattern of red, yellow, and gold autumn leaves that was almost an exact replica of the cross-stitch design on a set of place mats that my mother set on our table every Thanksgiving. My memory stirred, I gave the page a closer look and soon found my curiosity piqued by the idea of making my own clock. I called the company and put in an order that very day.

As I waited for my kit to arrive, I began to look into the whole craft of clockmaking, the art of turning everyday objects into clock faces. I discovered that clocks can be made from pieces of china, from photographs, from all sorts of needlecrafts, from paintings, drawings, and even treasured memorabilia. In essence, if you can drill a small hole in it for attaching the clockworks, you can make a clock out of it. The key to the ease of this craft is the pre-made, store-bought clockworks which are available at most stores that sell basic crafting supplies. Kits are also available for many clockmaking crafts, particularly those that involve needlework. One of the neatest ideas I came across was to take a favorite old china plate—perhaps the last of a set, or a single plate found at a flea market—and turn it into a clock face. This particular clock requires only a china plate, a drill with a ceramic bit, and some store-bought clockworks. I can imagine such a clock being the perfect addition to a kitchen or dining room's decor. I also came across clocks made from framed wedding invitations, perfect gifts for newlyweds; clocks made from souvenirs of favorite vacations; and charming little clocks made with children's artwork as the clock face. Each clock can be assembled with clockworks and the appropriate drill and bit for the material at hand. The more I learned about clockmaking, the more the idea appealed to me. Making a clock is a unique and meaningful way of preserving, presenting, and celebrating a piece of artwork or other treasured item.

As promised, my cross-stitch kit came complete with everything needed to make a clock—from the floss for the stitching to the frame for hanging and, of course, the clockworks and clear, detailed instructions for assembly. The process was indeed quite simple, with most of the work being in the stitching and framing, both of which were familiar to me from past projects. This particular kit did not even require drilling to attach the clockworks; they fit neatly and simply into a pre-made hole in the fabric and backing material. Assembling my clock was so trouble free that I was almost surprised when I first saw the elegant brass hands of the clock start moving; I guess until then I was hesitant to believe that I could actually put together a working clock.

While I was stitching my autumn leaves, I let my memory wander back in time to childhood Thanksgivings. For me, Thanksgiving has always been an evocative season. Without fail, this holiday brings on a warm and wonderful flow of memory. My Thanksgiving recollections are the peaceful, unspectacular sort, for Thanksgiving was never an elaborate celebration at our house. It was a quiet, family holiday.

Nor does Thanksgiving come at a particularly splendid time of the year where I grew up in north coastal Massachusetts. Although the stereotypical New England Thanksgiving scene involves trees aglow with glorious color, the truth is that by the end of November there is only one color left, and that is brown. A few dead leaves clinging to the bare branches are the extent of the foliage by the time Thanksgiving Thursday rolls around. Maybe that is why my mother loved those bright orange cross-stitch place mats with the vibrant leaves of earlier autumn days stitched upon them. They defied the drabness of the outdoors and helped her create a welcoming Thanksgiving season inside the walls of her home.

At work on my clock, awash in memories, I could almost smell the apple pies baking in my mother's kitchen. School always let out early on the Wednesday before Thanksgiving and I would come home, often through a raw fall rain, occasionally through a weakened November sun, to find my mother peeling and coring apples and rolling out pie crusts on the kitchen table. In the oven would be the scraps of crust she had formed into fun shapes and coated with cinnamon and sugar for an afternoon snack. I looked forward to those afternoons sitting at the table with my mother as she made her pies. I felt close to her, safe and secure and happy. The scene comes back easily to mind: the plastic tablecloth covered with flour for rolling out crusts, the colorful cardboard turkey that was always pinned to the back door, and, waiting in a neat stack for the next day's meal, the bright orange place mats with the cross-stitched autumn leaves. My mother's mother had stitched them herself and passed them along to become a signature part of our family Thanksgivings.

Now that my cross-stitch clock is completed, I have found a place for it in my kitchen. It hangs there today as Thanksgiving approaches and helps me mark the hours of my day. Now that I have discovered the ease of clockmaking, I plan to delve further into the craft. I imagine clocks as gifts for friends, as keepsakes for our family, as unique displays for the children's craft projects. But for now I am happy with my first clock, excited to have discovered a new craft, a new creative outlet, and happy to have a sweet and dependable reminder of a warm and happy time in my past.

So Little Time

Viney Wilder

There is so little time to feel the rain,
To hear the wind, to touch the cold white snow,
To look on ripened fields of golden grain,
To walk with April down a furrowed row.

So little time for toil and tears and mirth,
For joy and sorrow, pain and ecstasy,
For sowing seeds beneath the warm brown earth
And reaping harvests in humility.

So little time to dream, to think, to feel,
To linger with the stars when night is old,
To light a candle where the heart may kneel
In gratitude for blessings manifold.

But briefer yet by far the precious time
Left to the dreamer weaving words in rhyme.

Time and Wishes

Anona McConaghy

I wish that I could hold within my hand
The great hourglass
Of time, to close the fingers on the sand
And let it pass
To please my mood, to lay aside an hour
Of springtime bloom
To live again with heart uplifting power
In winter gloom.
I wish that I could savor ecstasy,
Stay pain's advance,
Or else tip back the frame that there might be
A second chance.
But earth's old clock, the moon, is still a sign
That time remains in wiser hands than mine.

Friends share some time lakeside in ANGLERS FISHING BY A LAKE
by Walton F. Image from Christie's Images.

LEGENDARY AMERICANS

Amy Johnson

JULIA MORGAN

Nestled in the Santa Lucia Mountains halfway between San Francisco and Los Angeles, in a quiet village called San Simeon, stands a masterpiece. A sprawling ranch covering 420 square miles boasts a 165-room mansion with fine furnishings, sculptures, and artwork from around the world, an immense meeting room with a table long enough to seat forty people, elaborate fireplaces, ornate ceilings, and Gothic windows. Surrounding the mansion are three guesthouses and two swimming pools, one of which is more than a hundred feet long and is accessible by a grand staircase that leads from one of the guesthouses to the blue water below. The entire project spanned more than eighteen years and cost almost five million dollars. Unlike the mansion, however, its designer was anything but ostentatious. The masterpiece at San Simeon was entirely designed by a quiet, unassum-

ing woman who stood no more than five feet tall. Her name was Julia Morgan.

Julia Morgan was born in San Francisco, California, in January of 1872. Even as a child, Julia was quiet and shy. She studied hard in school but enjoyed spending her free time playing outdoors with her four siblings. Julia looked forward to visiting her mother's relatives in New York every few summers. One of these relatives was Pierre LeBrun, a skilled architect who had designed the Metropolitan Life Insurance Tower in New York City. LeBrun recognized Julia's talent in mathematics and drawing, and it was his support and encouragement that inspired Julia to consider a career in architecture.

After graduating from Oakland High School in 1890, Julia entered the University of California at Berkeley, where she studied civil engineering. She became the first woman to receive a Bachelor of Science degree in civil engineering from the university. Julia then privately studied architecture and design under Bernard Maybeck, a teacher at Berkeley, for two years; and in the spring of 1896 she went to Paris to apply for admission to the École des Beaux-Arts, an elite architectural institution. The school had never admitted a woman, but this did not deter Julia in the least, even though the entrance exam would be administered in French. Julia took the exam in July of 1897; although her mastery of architecture and French was evident, she committed some critical errors using the metric system and was graded harshly by her examiners, who did not want to admit a woman to their program. She took the entrance exam twice more before finally passing in October of 1898. At about this time Julia met Phoebe Apperson Hearst, the mother of newspaper publisher and business tycoon William Randolph Hearst. Mrs. Hearst had financed a competition the previous year to help the University of California find a new design for its campus. Julia's former teacher, Bernard Maybeck, had spoken highly of Julia to Mrs. Hearst; and the following year, Mrs. Hearst visited Julia in Paris. A friendship began between the two women which would last for many years.

In December of 1901, Julia Morgan completed her coursework at the École des Beaux-Arts; she was the first woman to receive the certificate of study in architecture from the institution. She returned to California in early 1902, at the age of thirty, to begin her career in architecture. Julia began working for John Galen Howard, a New York architect who had also studied at the École des Beaux-Arts. Julia's first job for Howard was to design several buildings for her alma mater, the University of California at Berkeley. Although Julia enjoyed the work, she disliked the treatment she received from Howard and his other employees. Morgan's co-workers were pleasant toward her, but they did not believe that a woman could be a good architect. Howard recognized Julia's ability, yet he bragged about having an excellent worker whom he could pay "almost nothing, as it is a woman."

Julia believed in herself, and she knew she could succeed as an architect on her own. She opened an office in San Francisco and soon began to remodel the Hacienda, Phoebe Hearst's estate at Pleasanton, California. Morgan designed several large, elegant rooms for the house and added a swimming pool surrounded by glass doors. Mrs. Hearst was so pleased with Morgan's work on the Hacienda that she suggested the architect contact the Young Women's Christian Association (YWCA), which was looking for someone to design a conference facility in Pacific Grove, California. Morgan designed the building and entrance gates to the Asilomar Conference Center, as well as the administrative offices and a large central meeting area. Around this time, Morgan also designed a bell tower called El Campanil for Mills College, a school for women near Oakland. The tower stood seventy-five feet, was designed in the California Mission style of the eighteenth century, and was made of reinforced concrete to ensure against the earthquakes which were common to the area.

Only two years after the tower was built, a powerful earthquake shook the San Francisco bay area. The luxurious Fairmont Hotel was damaged by the quake. Upon learning that the tower at Mills College had withstood the earthquake, the owners of the Fairmont commissioned Morgan to restore the hotel. Along with her team of trained architects, Morgan successfully rebuilt the structure. As a result of her work on the Fairmont, Morgan gained recognition throughout the bay area and began to

earn the respect she deserved as an accomplished architect.

After the death of Phoebe Hearst in 1919, her son, William Randolph Hearst, entered Julia Morgan's office and asked her to begin work on his family's ranch at San Simeon. Hearst and his family divided their time between California and New York and had spent past summers at San Simeon camping in tents on a hill overlooking the ranch. Hearst hired Morgan to design a main house and three guesthouses at San Simeon, which sprawled over a staggering 270,000 acres. The main house, which he affectionately called "Casa Grande," was to be built in a combination of the classical European style Morgan had studied at the École des Beaux-Arts and the Spanish mission architecture that was prevalent in California. Julia drew up most of her plans for the mansion from her San Francisco office but willingly made the almost eight-hour trip to San Simeon on weekends during the actual building process to oversee the work there.

Between 1919 and 1932, Julia Morgan devoted her time to the work at San Simeon. At its peak in the 1930s, San Simeon included a private zoo and was visited by entertainers Charlie Chaplain and Greta Garbo, among others. Financial setbacks slowed work at San Simeon in the late 1930s, and the onset of World War II hurt Morgan's other business projects as building materials became scarce and several members of Morgan's architectural staff were called to serve in the armed forces. By 1950, a series of small strokes had taken their toll on Morgan, and she was forced to close her San Francisco office. She spent the last years of her life surrounded by her family and died on February 2, 1957, at the age of eighty-five. Despite the fact that Morgan was instrumental to the elaborate work at San Simeon, she never sought fame or fortune throughout her life. In the only interview she ever gave, after her successful completion of the Fairmont Hotel, Morgan stressed that her job was to let her buildings speak for her. "Architecture," she said, "is a visual, not a verbal art." Morgan left a legacy through her work that lives on today, not only in the magnificent Hearst Castle at San Simeon, but also through her silent example to let her buildings show the world that she was indeed an architect who influenced history.

HEARST CASTLE
SAN SIMEON, CALIFORNIA

Elizabeth Bonner Kea

During my final year of college, I decided to add some variety to my course load by taking an art-history class entitled "Great American Homes: an overview of the history, architecture, and preservation of America's domestic treasures." As a history buff with a love for travel and architecture, how could I pass on such a class? Over the next few weeks, I learned of Mount Vernon, the Biltmore, Monticello, and other magnifient homesteads; but none so amazed me as Hearst Castle in San Simeon, California. Encompassing more than 250,000 acres that included one main house, three guesthouses, and countless garden walks, the "castle" had size that rivaled, if not surpassed, most other homes included in my course; and I knew I would one day have to experience San Simeon's grandeur for myself.

It was not until a few years later, while visiting a friend in California, that I fulfilled my desire. My friend and I set off down the Pacific Coastline from San Francisco to enjoy two days at Hearst Castle. During our drive, I pulled out a guidebook to refresh my memory on some of the estate's fascinating history and prepare my friend for what lay in store. In the 1920s, "Camp Hill," as the acreage was once called, was owned by business entrepreneur William Randolph Hearst. Wanting to make his camp more comfortable, he contacted San Francisco architect Julia Morgan. He explained: "Miss Morgan, we are tired of camping out in the open at the ranch in San Simeon, and I would like to build a little something." Morgan accepted his proposal; and over the next eighteen years the "little something" Hearst envisioned became Hearst Castle, an estate of more than ninety thousand square feet.

Even after reading this history and quoting the measurements of Hearst Castle to my friend, I was not prepared for the castle's sheer massiveness and beauty once it sprawled before us. We first toured a portion of the 127 acres of walkways, gardens, and terraces that cross the estate. We meandered through gardens inspired by the great Italian and Spanish gardens of Europe and enjoyed magnificent views of mountains and coastline just as Hearst's guests had done more than half a century ago. A pathway led us up the hillside to one of Hearst Castle's three guesthouses, Casa del Sol. As we climbed the stairs to the house's entrance, we noticed the stark white Mediterranean Revival architecture framed against the blue sky. Several yards away, we could look over one of the estate's two spectacular pools, the Neptune Pool, appropriately named for its Greco-Roman style. Later, we were also able to see the indoor Roman Pool, which was surrounded by colorful floor-to-ceiling tile mosaics that were modeled after fifth-century designs in Ravenna, Italy.

What my friend and I had experienced so far on our tour was building up to what I considered Hearst Castle's most impressive sight, the Casa Grande, or main house, which we visited on the second day of our trip. With thirty-eight bedrooms, forty-one bathrooms, and more than sixty thousand square feet of living space, the home was indeed grand; and its imposing towers and Spanish cathedral architecture announce that status to all who approach its doors. As I entered, I marveled at the finery that Hearst afforded his friends and family, and I could hardly imagine what it would have been like to be an actual invited guest. The Assembly Room boasted carved mahogany walls and a marble fireplace where Hearst's visitors were known to gather at all hours. In the Library, they could browse through more than four thousand books and a collection of rare Greek and Roman antiquities, and the Morning Room surrounded them with Spanish antiques and Flemish

An entrance to the Hearst Castle reveals a hint of its grandeur. Photo by Superstock.

tapestries. In fact, almost every room held a portion of Hearst's vast European and Mediterranean art collection that led one world-renowned architectural historian to say that "Hearst Castle is a palace in every sense of the word."

As my friend and I finished our tour and drove away, I turned around for one last glimpse of *La Cuesta Encantada,* or Enchanted Hill, as Hearst affectionately called it. I was sorry we had had only

two days to spend exploring the estate, but in this short time I already felt as if I had truly been the guest of William Hearst. I may not have actually swam alongside the statues at the Roman Pool or enjoyed after-dinner conversation in the Morning Room, but all the architecture, history, beauty, and grandeur of Hearst Castle had been mine to experience and enjoy.

Abundance

Margaret Rorke

The abundance of the season,
With its store of winter food,
Was the underlying reason
For the Pilgrims' grateful mood.
By our standards it was meager;
By our plenty it was bare;
But that little band was eager
To thank Him who'd put it there.

With abundance we're surrounded;
We have endless sky and sea.
By no limits are we bounded
But the wills of you and me.
There is friendship, there is beauty,
There is courage, faith, and hope.
These impose no mortal duty;
They are infinite in scope.

For abundance found in living,
For the very gift of life,
Let us voice on this Thanksgiving
Above the stridency of strife
Our sincere appreciation
Unto Him to whom it's due;
So He'll know His favored nation
Has a heart abundant too.

The Twenty-Fourth Psalm

Margaret Rorke

"The earth is the Lord's and the fullness thereof,"
Sang the psalmist in worship of old.
And the pilgrims used this as their paean of love
On Thanksgiving, so we have been told.

They were thankful for life. They were thankful for food.
They were thankful for finding this sod.
Here their people could be where the worship was free;
For all this they were thankful to God.

On this day when we pause, when we gather to feast,
When we're counting our labor's rewards,
It is well we recall what's oft lost with the least:
That the earth and its gifts are the Lord's.

A floral-bedecked dining room awaits Thanksgiving dinner.
Photo by Jessie Walker.

FOREVER AT HOME

Craig Wilson

The farmhouse my great-grandparents built at the turn of the century in upstate New York passed out of the family this month. It was bought by a man I do not know.

Family legend has it that my great-grandfather was furious at the builders when the final price tag in 1901 came in at $3,900, double the initial estimate.

But for that price, he got a house so big, so tall, and so massive that painters sometimes balked at taking on the job of giving it a fresh coat of white.

By the time I arrived on the scene, it was home to my grandmother, my aunt and uncle, and my cousins. Just up the road, a five-minute walk away, it was my second home.

It never crossed my mind growing up that one day a Wilson wouldn't live there anymore. After all, my dad was born in an upstairs bedroom. His grandfather and father were laid out in the front parlor, the same room where we celebrated Christmas Eve every year. But as a kid, you never think that times change, that people move on, that very often life offers up circumstances beyond anyone's control.

Most of us of a certain age have such a place in our pasts. Usually a grandparent's house, the kind not built anymore. Big, with heavy storm windows that had to be removed in the spring, and wood screen doors that banged with every coming and going on a hot summer's day.

Architecturally, the house was an elephant. Lumbering, ponderous, yet somehow comforting. The attic was bigger than most people's homes, and there were so many rooms upstairs, an inquisitive child could spend years exploring them, and did.

There were front stairs off the living room and back stairs off the kitchen and steep stairs to the cool, stone-walled cellar where rainwater was collected in a cistern. And there were porches—front, back, and side. There even was a porch off a bedroom upstairs; it could be reached only by climbing out the window.

There was a front door, too, but it was knocked on only by traveling salesmen. Everyone else came in through the kitchen, where plants filled the windows.

Not that the place didn't have its eccentricities. A downstairs bathroom was so cold, you never lingered long in the winter, and the water pressure in the upstairs bathroom was so poor that you couldn't shower. The shower was in the cellar, used by my uncle and cousin when they came in from the orchards.

There was a huge wood-paneled pantry, and a glass-door kitchen cupboard that went right through to the dining room, a feature I thought quite inventive at the time.

And then there were the smells. Glorious smells.

The kitchen during canning season, when applesauce was strained through an old metal sieve; the mudroom in winter, when it reeked of wet wool; the stairway to my grandmother's quarters, where the scent of furniture polish mingled with fresh chocolate chip cookies and the faint smell of the perfume she always wore.

Gone, yes, along with the house.

But very much still here.

APPLE BUTTER
Anne Campbell

It takes a woman's hands to lock
Such sweetness in an old brown crock
Cooled in a springhouse made of rock—
Apple butter.

It tastes of clover blossoms fanned
By winds that fell upon the land;
Of pinks and phlox, you understand?
Apple butter.

The apple tree threw out its shade.
Its roots grew deeply in the glade.
From crimson harvest we had made
Apple butter.

And when I eat it now I see
The mellow arms of that old tree
That generously gave to me
Apple butter.

Once more across the table's space
I smile into a lovely face
And share with her, in my old place,
Apple butter.

I guess I'm like the tree that bore
These apples, finding more and more
My roots grown deep in time's rich store.
Pass me—and open childhood's door—
Apple butter.

APPLE BUTTER
Jessie Cannon Eldridge

So smooth, the spreading of this apple treat.
Roll back the winter, see the apples grow
Red on the tree, so very good to eat,
So fine for buttering. Sit here and know
The gift of giving is a lovely thing,
And lovelier, the dear remembering.

The day's harvest promises delicious apple butter in
POMMES DANS UN PANIER ET SUR LA TABLE *by Henri Fantin-Latour.*
Image from Christie's Images.

COLLECTOR'S CORNER

TABLE LINENS
Laurie Hunter

When I was young, I paid little attention to domestic details. Nevertheless, the things I didn't seem to notice when I was a child are just the things I remember clearly as an adult, particularly at this time of year when I think back to holiday meals. Surely everyone's table was laden with a glistening turkey or sugar-crusted ham accompanied with all the trimmings, from heaping bowls of buttered yams to baskets of piping hot rolls. Strange salads were also no doubt a staple in which both fruit and vegetables blended together as if they too were joining the family reunion.

My family's feast was unique, however, because it was always spread across the same backdrop—mother's sage-green, dressy tablecloth with a pleasingly knotted fringe. Thirty-something years later, I still travel to Mother's house for the holidays. I pack my family into the car and roam three hundred miles, spurred on by the knowledge that Mother's table will look exactly the same.

One might think her old tablecloth belongs in the attic by now. But I believe that the past is just as at home in the present. Like any heirloom, the tablecloth improves with age. It doesn't matter what dishes Mother prepares, either the traditional favorites or new recipes to enliven the ageless celebration; the "tradition" is captured when she spreads that green tablecloth across her table.

I found myself amazed at how a piece of fabric could end up as a cherished fragment of my memory. So when family members, seemingly on a whim, began to discard their old table linens in yard sales and the like, I became quite adamant in rescuing them. I eventually found myself adopting linen cast-offs until I had quite a historical collection. It includes a pink cotton tablecloth with eight matching napkins that Grandmama set aside in favor of more modern table dressings when she moved to her new house. An avocado-green, hand-crocheted, oval tablecloth I saved from my mother's yard sale. A cheery, red-and-white square luncheon cloth that accompanied our family on Sunday picnics. The off-white, Jacquard-weave, damask cloth that graced one of the tables at our wedding reception. Hand-embroidered bread basket liners that had been my cousin's. A yellow gingham cloth that was always draped over a card table whenever we had more guests than the dining table could hold. Pleated, pine-green place mats for Christmas. And a chintz table runner that belonged to my "two times great" Aunt.

But my collection doesn't stop there. Naturally, I also had to make room for other table linens I found along the way, nostalgic ones that simply reminded me of my family. I'd see one at an antique mall or yard sale and think, "We used to have a tablecloth just like this." Then of course I'd have to take it home.

My love for fabrics wasn't planned. It just happened. The more table linens I acquired, the more I liked them. Carefully folded and stacked into piles or neatly rolled and tucked into remaining narrow gaps, linen curiosities now completely fill the cedar shelves of my linen closet, and with them, folds of my family's life story. Interestingly enough, their texture only grows softer, more touchable, and more beautiful with time.

Whenever I'm expecting relatives, I'll open the cabinet and select a few favorites, one for the formal dining room as well as something for the sideboard. Even the breakfast table dons a new gown. When the guests arrive, they immediately feel welcomed by the familiarity of the often-forgotten table linens. "Didn't I have a tablecloth just like this?" "Weren't these Grandmama's place mats?" "These napkins always remind me of summer." Stories start circulating. Laughter kicks in. Distance and time are quickly erased. All because of a piece of cloth. No wonder we call it "the fabric of our lives."

SET FOR SERVICE

If you would like to collect vintage table linens, the following information may be helpful.

TABLE LINEN BASICS

• Table linens make great collectibles because they are useful, beautiful, affordable and can be passed down through the ages. Vintage textiles, although more difficult to find than newer versions, are definitely worth the search. Each hints at a past era and former family get-togethers.

• The term *table linens* typically refers to table-cloths as well as cloth place mats, table runners, and napkins. These are available in a vast assortment of sizes. For example, napkins include standard dinner napkins; smaller tea or cocktail napkins; and banquet-sized "lapkins."

• Table linens also include refreshment or luncheon sets, which consist of square table "covers" and matching square napkins. Other table linens include chairback doilies, aprons, bread basket liners, silverware wrappings, and tea cozies.

• Contemporary and vintage table linens are available in a variety of colors, patterns, textures, shapes, and fabrics.

• Fabric choices include lace, muslin, linen, cotton, organdy, rayon, burlap, and cambric.

• Linens can be adorned with embroidery, hemstitching, scalloped edges, box corners, beads, buttons, hand-initialed monograms, crocheted patterns, and many other decorative designs and stitching techniques.

POPULAR PICKS

• Popular colors for table linens in the 1930s, 40s, and 50s included jade green, turquoise, and strawberry red. By the 60s and 70s, colors were becoming more subdued. Earth tones included brown, mustard, moss, and orange swirled into a variety of geometrical patterns.

• Souvenir tablecloths from the mid-twentieth century, sporting popular vacation hot spots and travel motifs, have recently gained popularity.

• Holiday table linens can often be found in mint condition because they were rarely used.

A collection of table linens offers a history of family celebrations. Photo by Rick Lance. Linens courtesy Shamiran Prater and Linda Butts.

CARING FOR LINENS

• It is best to merely spot clean antique linens. Spills should be treated immediately by dabbing the cloth with a weak solution of water and a gentle stain remover.

• If total laundering is necessary, use gentle detergents in the washing machine or pure soap flakes if washing by hand. For extremely delicate or intricately fringed pieces, tuck the textiles into a lingerie bag or pillowcase before washing.

• Dry cleaning is not recommended for vintage linens, and line drying is preferred.

• For storage, consider a dry, clean, well-ventilated location that protects fabric from harsh sunlight. To prevent creases, layer linens between sheets of acid-free tissue and roll onto acid-free tubes. Do not, however, store your table linens in plastic (which prevents air circulation) or with potpourri sachets (which can cause fabrics that are not used frequently to deteriorate).

Frequent Mishap

Grace V. Watkins

Our Aunt Miranda never was a great
Success at baking bread, for always she
Would meet with some uncalculated fate
Before the loaves were done. So finally we
Grew reconciled to hearing that the day
Was much too warm, the yeast a trifle old,
The oven wasn't working quite the way
It should, or that the flour bin was cold.
And yet, for all the mishaps that befell,
We children counted it next door to bliss
To eat a slice covered with cherry jell.
And one of childhood's great delights was this:
To watch our Aunt Miranda sigh and cut
A snowy loaf that would have been great—but!

Brown bread and the
gospel are good fare.

——Puritan saying

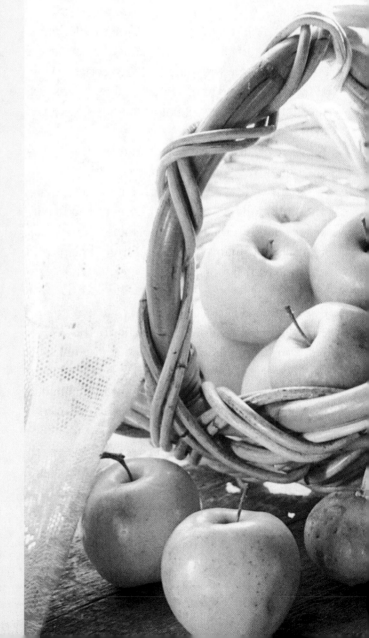

The scent of a fresh loaf of bread calls the family to the table.
Photo by Nancy Matthews.

Family Recipes

To add warmth and tradition to your family get-together, nothing beats a well-loved bread recipe passed down through the generations. These are some of our readers' family favorites. We would love to try your favorite recipe too. Send a typed copy to Ideals Publications, 535 Metroplex Drive, Suite 250, Nashville, TN 37211. We pay $10 for each recipe published.

Zucchini Bread
Norma George of Louisville, Ohio

3 cups all-purpose flour
1½ teaspoons baking powder
1 teaspoon baking soda
1 teaspoon salt
3 teaspoons ground cinnamon
2½ cups granulated sugar
2 cups zucchini,
    unpeeled and finely chopped
1 teaspoon vanilla
3 eggs, beaten
1 cup vegetable oil
1 cup nuts, chopped

Preheat oven to 350° F. In a large bowl, sift together flour, baking powder, baking soda, salt, and cinnamon. Set aside. In a large bowl, combine sugar, zucchini, vanilla, and eggs; add oil and beat well. Slowly stir in dry ingredients. Fold in nuts. Pour batter into 2 greased loaf pans. Bake 1 hour or until toothpick inserted in center comes out clean. Makes 2 loaves.

Dressed-Up Corn Bread
Chris Horne of Macon, Georgia

1 cup plain meal
½ cup self-rising flour
1 teaspoon baking powder
1 tablespoon granulated sugar
⅛ teaspoon salt
½ cup English walnuts, chopped
9 slices bacon, cooked and crumbled
1 egg
1 cup milk
¼ cup vegetable oil

Preheat oven to 400° F. In a large bowl, sift together meal, flour, baking powder, sugar, and salt. Stir in nuts and bacon; set aside. In a medium bowl, beat egg. Add milk slowly, then add oil. Slowly stir in dry ingredients; mix well. Spoon into buttered iron skillet. Bake 20 minutes or until golden. Makes 8 servings.

Boston Brown Bread

Helen Storch of Davenport, Iowa

1 cup raisins
½ cup plus 1 tablespoon
 all-purpose flour, divided
2 teaspoons baking soda

1 teaspoon salt
2 cups whole wheat flour
2 cups buttermilk
½ cup dark molasses

Preheat oven to 350° F. Remove labels from and grease well two 5¼-inch by 3¾-inch coffee cans (13-ounce size) and set aside. Place raisins in a small bowl and cover with hot water; set aside. In a large bowl, combine flour, baking soda, and salt. Set aside. In a separate large bowl, combine whole wheat flour, buttermilk, and molasses.

Add to first flour mixture and mix well. Drain raisins, mix with 1 tablespoon flour, and fold into batter. Pour batter into prepared coffee cans. Bake 45 to 50 minutes or until toothpick inserted into center comes out clean. Cool in pan; turn onto wire rack. Makes 2 loaves.

Bill's Pumpkin Bread

Wanda Tucker of McAlester, Oklahoma

3⅓ cups all-purpose flour
2 teaspoons baking soda
½ teaspoon salt
1 tablespoon ground cinnamon
4 eggs
1 cup vegetable oil

⅓ cup water
1 15-ounce can pumpkin
3 cups granulated sugar
½ cup chopped dates
½ cup chopped nuts

Preheat oven to 350° F. In a large bowl, sift together flour, baking soda, salt, and cinnamon. Set aside. In a large bowl, beat eggs well. Add oil, water, and pumpkin. Stir in sugar. Slowly stir in dry ingredients. Fold in dates and nuts. Pour batter

into 2 greased and floured loaf pans. Bake 1 hour to 1 hour and 15 minutes or until toothpick inserted into center comes out clean. Cool in pan 10 minutes; turn onto wire rack. Makes 2 loaves.

THROUGH MY WINDOW

Pamela Kennedy

Art by Meredith Johnson

THANKSGIVING LEFTOVERS

It's a couple of weeks before Thanksgiving, and my plate is already full. I have deadlines at work, company coming, a house to clean, commitments at church, and a writing project due. I am not looking forward to planning and putting on a Thanksgiving dinner, and I haven't been silent about my concerns.

"I have a great idea," my helpful husband suggests one evening. "Let's go out this Thanksgiving. Look here."

He whips out the entertainment section of the newspaper and sets it before me with a flourish. Apparently the public relations departments of several businesses in our town have recognized there's a big market in overwhelmed homemakers this time of year.

"Let us do your cooking!" one ad coaxes.

"Why face a mountain of dirty dishes?" another

ad queries.

"You can be thankful you don't have to worry this holiday season!" promises another.

A luxury hotel invites us to eat and sleep over at their place: "You be our guest this Thanksgiving weekend!"

I'm not too sure about my husband's plan. I think there is something vaguely un-American about going out for Thanksgiving dinner. I wonder about this out loud, but he assures me I would be breaking no unwritten laws. Besides, he adds, he will certainly be grateful that I'm not frazzled and overwhelmed with all the Thanksgiving preparations.

I look once more at the stack of papers I have to correct, the dust in the guest room, and my calendar. "Okay, let's do it." We decide upon an "All-you-can-eat traditional Thanksgiving dinner complete with seven side dishes and homemade pumpkin pie."

Reservations are secured, and I place a bold check mark next to "Thanksgiving" on my to-do list!

In a long-distance phone conversation with my mother-in-law a week later, she asks what our plans are for Thanksgiving.

"We're going out!" I announce triumphantly.

"Oh, to a friend's home?" she inquires.

"No, to a restaurant."

"A restaurant?" she repeats. There's a short pause. "But you won't have any leftovers," she eventually adds.

"Yes, that's true, and there also won't be any shopping, cooking, working, worrying, or clean up. Personally I think it's a pretty good trade-off," I counter with a laugh.

"I suppose so. It's just that I really love leftovers," she says wistfully.

Long after our conversation ends, her comments linger in my thoughts. Leftovers? What an odd thing to be concerned about.

Thanksgiving Day we spend a lazy morning visiting with our houseguests. We linger over a second cup of coffee and decide to take a drive through some of the local scenic areas. I have no turkey to baste or pies to bake, no table to set, potatoes to mash, or yams to glaze. I'm free from all that, and I feel almost giddy.

At about three o'clock in the afternoon we drive to our Thanksgiving dinner appointment. An elegantly attired maitre d' welcomes us and guides us to our table. It's set with gleaming silver and china and small cornucopias filled with miniature pumpkins and gourds. Soon we're feasting on succulent slices of turkey smothered in gravy. Our accompaniments include mounds of fluffy mashed potatoes, savory dressing, yams in pecan and caramel glaze, fresh fruit salad, green beans with almonds, and creamed onions. Conversation ebbs and flows around soft classical music as efficient waiters fill and refill our plates and glasses. When the pumpkin pie arrives, few of us can resist although we're feeling as stuffed as the turkey must have been.

After a short walk in the balmy evening, we return home. I notice how orderly the kitchen looks when I enter it later to set up the coffee pot for breakfast. There are no pots and pans filled with half-congealed turkey and gravy, no stacks of dishes and silver waiting to be washed, no containers of dressing, potatoes, or vegetables crowding the counters. There are no leftovers.

With the house quiet and everyone settled in for the night, I make a cup of tea and sit at the kitchen table. How odd that my mother-in-law's words echo in my mind. Sipping from the steaming cup, I smile remembering how I'd sneak downstairs after Thanksgiving dinner when I was a little girl to enjoy a rich baked turkey wing. And on the day after Thanksgiving my favorite breakfast was a slice of cold pumpkin pie smothered in whipped cream. Mother had a regular retinue of post-Thanksgiving dinners almost as traditional as the holiday feast. Friday we'd have hot turkey sandwiches. Saturday was turkey chow mein. Sunday would be turkey-noodle casserole, and by Monday night we were on to turkey vegetable soup. But there were other leftovers too—leftover memories of preparing the bird for the oven, setting the table with special decorations made by the children, a kitchen filled with scents of spices, baking turkey and steaming gravy, prayers said in the candlelight around a table filled with family and friends. Men argued over the execution of a football play, and kitchen conversations swirled around family events. These were all leftovers too.

In my quiet and uncluttered solitude I was rested and serene, but I was also without leftovers: those treasured remnants of a holiday come and gone. It was nice to have this time to reflect, but I also felt a small stab of disappointment when I opened the refrigerator later and observed its tidy contents. Tomorrow, I decided, I'd make a pumpkin pie. And if there were a piece left over, I'd have it for breakfast on Saturday. Maybe next year I'll try to manage my time a little better. We could have some people in for Thanksgiving dinner. Everyone could bring something to share. It wouldn't be too much work for anyone and there would be plenty to eat. And best of all, we could each have lots of leftovers!

Pamela Kennedy is a freelance writer of short stories, articles, essays, and children's books. Wife of a retired naval officer and mother of three children, she has made her home on both U.S. coasts and currently resides in Honolulu, Hawaii.

TODAY, I GIVE THANKS

Grace Barnette Lucas

The one sturdy rose bloom left alone
In a garden where scarlet leaves have blown.
The crisp freshness of the morning air;
The bright gold of mums so fair.
The warm fireside that glows
As outside the north wind blows.
The aroma of turkey, yams, and cakes;
The spicy pumpkin pie that bakes.
The love of family, friends so dear,
The laughter of my children near.
The church's steeple rising high,
The songs we sing, the prayers we sigh.
For all the little things in life,
The love that overcomes all strife,
These are the things for which I say,
"I thank You" to my Lord today.

DAILY THANKSGIVING

Beatrice Munro Wilson

I thank Thee, Lord, for daily things—
The song a little wild bird sings,
Misty asters on the hills,
Geraniums on windowsills,

For dewdrop jewels angels spill
When the dawn is cool and still,
For laughing child and romping pup,
For cold, sweet water in my cup,

First snowdrop, and fall wind's caress,
A friend's warm hand in time of stress,
For work to do, for rain and sun,
And quiet rest when day is done,

For blue woodsmoke and firelit pane,
For surety spring will come again.
For each day's sweets and eyes that see,
Father, I thank You, joyously.

*Richly colored trees frame a steeple in Concord, Massachusetts.
Photo by Dianne Dietrich Leis/Dietrich Stock Photo.*

AGAINST THE COLD

Ruth B. Field

The huge copper kettle's heaped with logs;
The flames leap high as evening shadows fall
And in the friendly dusk of the room
Make fanciful dark patterns on the wall.
The lacquered moon sails high across the sky;
Frost fingers make a trail across the earth.
But where the fire sends spark showers high,
There is no cold about the ruddy hearth.
The autumn nights grow chill; forgotten dreams
Return beside the fire's glowing embers.
No chill can penetrate where brightly gleams
Sweet memories the heart fondly remembers.

ON BUILDING A WOOD FIRE

Glenn Ward Dresbach

In youth we seemed to think the greatest pile
Of any wood at all was our desire,
Just so it crackled loudly for a while—
Though we could not get very near the fire.
But after we had time enough, we learned
To gather less wood, chosen more and more
To last and give a fragrance while it burned—
And we crouched closer to it than before.

We built for less smoke and for steady flame
And shielded it from wind, enough to hold
Its place a secret—unless someone came
Into its circle from the dark or cold—
Drawn by a fragrance drifting on the air—
And stretched the hands to warmth the heart may share.

*Artist Judy Gibson depicts the ideal place to escape the chilly
autumn air in* Cozy Cabin. *Image copyright © Arts Uniq, Inc.,
Cookeville, Tennessee.*

Supper Time
Hilda Sanderson

Tired from all her
Willing work of spring
And summer's long and
Listful nurturing,
Mother Earth sees fall
As supper time,
Where upon fall's harvest
She will dine
Just before her sleep
In winter's breast,
Where after supper, finally,
She will rest.

Fall
Melissa Pinol

The old earth is changing;
The seasons turn round.
The autumn leaves flutter
Their way to the ground.

My own world is changing;
The seasons conspire
To grant me the peace
Of a rest by the fire.

A picnic area overlooks a golden vineyard near
Forest Grove, Oregon. Photo by Steve Terrill.

A Harvest for Me

Matthew Wenke

In careful harvest I long for you to bring
A potpourri of pleasure, profuse and lingering.
Oh, gather one perfect autumn day for me
To treasure in the sunlit attic of my memory!

Bring crickets in chorus, that joyful evening din,
Cold apple cider, and a jack-o'-lantern's grin.
Bring haunting winds to precede a frosty dawn
And acorns and oak leaves to scatter on the lawn.

Don't forget Indian corn to hang on the door,
Freshly cleaned windows, canned goods in store,
The warm plaids and tweeds of jackets and caps,
The burlap stiffness of woolen underwraps.

Set purple asters to drying in a vase
With milkweed pods in a warm and sunny space.
Conjure roadside stands, their wares in woven bins,
And bushel baskets to gather hickory nuts in.

Bring shocks of cornstalks, standing dry and brown
In golden pastures; and geese leaving town.
Etch bright blue sky to accent overhead,
A leafy horizon of yellow, orange, and red.

Once my potpourri is gathered with care
And one perfect autumn day is collected in there,
Bind it with tenderness and place it for me
In the sunlit attic of my memory.

Harvest

Starrlette L. Howard

We cannot all own a garden
Or pantry behind a cellar door.
We can't all see the harvest
From seed to field to store.
Yet the golden days of harvest
And the goodness that you measure
Can be stored within your hearts
As your own supply of treasure.

Indian corn creates a wall of color in Willamette Valley, Oregon. Photo by Steve Terrill.

SEEDING TIME

Helen Virden

The silver milkweed pods split open now;
The asters shed their beauty far and near;
A mullin's seed turned under by the plow
Will fight its way to light another year.
A breath of winter wind shakes goldenrod
And brings that cobweb castle to the earth.
This is the way of life, the will of God,
To reproduce the summer's golden worth.

The autumn glory fades away and dies;
The heads of cotton grass drift white and brown.
And overall, a blessing in disguise,
The leaves of elms and maples flutter down.
The winter through long months will pray her beads,
White shawled, will rock and guard her nestled seeds.

*Milkweed seeds land atop a pile of red maple leaves
in Missouri. Photo by Gay Bumgarner.*

MOTHER IN THE KITCHEN

Marjorie Holmes

Mother was not an impassioned cook. She felt a defensive, half-guilty distress for women who spent most of their time in the kitchen. "All that work just for something to put in your mouth and swallow, just to fill your stomach, just to eat." To her, food for the soul was just as important, and she feasted richly, if indiscriminately, on Tennyson and Tarkington, Shakespeare and Grace Noll Crowell and Harold Bell Wright. She would often become so absorbed in a book that it would be late afternoon before she came to, shocked to discover from the redolent odors wafting up and down the block that other people's suppers were cooking. "Oh, dear, what'll we have?" she would worry vaguely, and start summoning offspring for calculations and tasks.

If in summer, someone would be dispatched to pick, pull, or dig whatever was ready from the garden, and fingers would fly, snapping, shelling, or peeling things. Meanwhile, she would achieve a small list of items for when the phone would ring and whoever was downtown would ask, "What do you want for supper?" Often she dismissed the whole business with a cheerful, "Oh, I don't care, just whatever looks good."

Dad didn't mind, and he bought with a lavish hand when he could. If times were plentiful the meat was invariably thick red beefsteak, and the sack would be full of surprises like Nabiscos and coconut-topped marshmallow cookies, along with cherry pie from the bakery, and white grapes. And maybe a fresh hairy coconut, which we broke open with a hammer, drinking its flat tasteless milk and prying out its sweet if tough white heart.

We were always ravenous by suppertime, and no matter what was served we fell on it with relish. Especially on the days when the bread was fresh from the oven. Though Mother would never win any ribbons at the county fair and didn't want to, she did make good bread. And like everybody else (except the elite who could afford the extravagance of bakery bread) she was forced to bake it once a week.

The batter had to be mixed and set to rise the night before. A great, yeasty, bubbling batch in a huge granite pan. Potato water was saved to combine with the scalded milk, salt, sugar, and lard, and into this she sifted white cones of flour. We often knelt on kitchen chairs to watch, begging to help by shaking the heavy, squeaking flour sifter. When the dough was thick and smooth, it was covered with a lid and left to rise on the lingering warmth at the back of the stove. If the house were cold, Mother would tuck the dough down as cozily as she could under a heavy towel.

By morning it would have blossomed tall and white, only to be stirred down and forced to accept more flour. Now she must dump it onto a floured board and knead it, flopping the tough yet delicate mass over and over, pressing out the air bubbles that made little squealing protests, caressing it, yet maneuvering it to her will. And thus subdued it was set to rise again.

By afternoon it was ready to be kneaded once more and molded into loaves. When we were small she always pinched off enough dough to let us play with and to fashion into tiny loaves of our own. They were usually grubby from our hands, but they looked beautiful waiting on the sunny windowsill in the little lids that served as pans. When the loaves themselves had risen, she brushed their plump heads with melted butter and popped them into an oven so hot that sometimes the lids on the range were as rosy as rouged cheeks.

Slowly the heavenly smell of baking bread began to drift through the house. When you came in from school or play your jaws leaked and you began to tease, "When will the bread be done?"

"Well, it should be soon." Opening the nickel-

The centerpiece of the supper table is met with smiles. Image from Superstock.

plated door, she would reach in and snap an experimental finger on the brown cracking crust. "Just a few more minutes." Finally, clutching a dish towel, she would reach in and carefully draw out the large black pan. The loaves were dumped on the table, to stand tall and golden as the sheaves of wheat from which the flour had come. Promptly she brushed them with more butter, and they took on a satin sheen. When she broke them apart, their white flesh steamed.

"Now don't eat too much," she would warn as people begged for more. "Hot bread isn't good for the stomach. Besides, I don't want you to spoil your supper."

On rare occasions she diverted part of the batch into cinnamon rolls, a special treat. But the fresh bread itself eaten straight from the oven with butter, or slavered with honey or strawberry jam or apple

butter, was enough to rouse the envy of the gods.

Mother also made a marvelous bread pudding dignified by the name of "chocolate soufflé." Dry bread soaked in scalded milk; sugar, cocoa, vanilla, and a couple of eggs added. Baked in a moderate oven until a knife came clean and its rich chocolaty promise was scarcely to be borne. The crowning touch was the hard sauce, which one of us always made. Confectioner's sugar was stirred into about half a cup of butter, added and pressed and added and pressed until you achieved a fat white ball that could literally take no more. (Also a few drops of vanilla.) Then you made it into individual balls, and stamped on each with the bottom of a cut-glass toothpick holder, the imprint of a diamond or a daisy or a star. Bread pudding? Nonsense. These creamy balls, melting down over each crusty steaming dish, achieved ambrosia.

Fourth Thursday
in November

Kunigunde Duncan

He sits backwards on the bird bath
As if scorning
Such a thing as bathing
This near-winter morning.
A thin skim of ice
Is on the water, he must know,
For he turns about and tests it
With a cautious toe.
Startled, taking wing,
To hear breaking ice clink,
He flutters, alights again,
Takes a brief drink,
Before he dives in
With beak and feather
In this most excellent
Bathing weather!
Shakes off the water,
Glad he's living,
And bursts into a cardinal's
Carol of thanksgiving.

A pair of doves enjoys the bathing weather in BIRD BATH
by Dr. Jeremy Paul. Image copyright © Arts Uniq, Inc.,
Cookeville, Tennessee.

Country CHRONICLE

Lansing Christman

THE NOVEMBER FURROW

The November furrow across the field is like a finger of the land pointing to something beyond the meadow's end, the wood's edge, or a line fence. It points beyond autumn to something deeper than the soil from which the plowshare turns the stubble and the sod.

I thought of these things the other day when I saw neighbors of mine plowing in their fields. When I was still a part-time farmer more than sixty years ago, we did our fall plowing in October and November, after we had hauled to the barn the shocks of corn and picked the apples from the orchard on the hill.

I like to think now, as I thought then, that the November furrow, glistening in the sun, means far more than a symbol of a harvest's end or the year's close. There would be no furrow across a field if man did not harbor the hope of year leading into year. A man, watching the share of the plow turn furrow after furrow to the sun, is building for another harvest in the year to come.

I have always been able to see beyond the November furrow, beyond winter's rain and ice and snow, beyond the biting winds. It is easy, even now, to envision the autumn furrow breathing in a March rain or the warmth of the April sun. I like to think the furrow moves uneasily, restless as a child of morning, waiting to awaken from its night of sleep.

The author of three books, Lansing Christman has contributed to Ideals *for almost thirty years. Mr. Christman has also been published in several American, foreign, and braille anthologies. He lives in rural South Carolina.*

A tractor plows a field below the bluffs of the Missouri hills.
Photo by Gay Bumgarner.

NOVEMBER

Helen Monnette

How can I forget thee, O November?
When skies are gray and days are cold and drear,
When snow goes racing over field and meadow,
And winter trailing thee so very near.

A few more leaves may wrangle and debate
And cling tenaciously to limb and bough,
But will by thy insistence leave the tree
And let thee bear them in their final hour

Down to the earth to nurture all the roots and seeds,
To die, and in dying, bring new life again
To all the many flowers and herbs and weeds
That in the earth lie dormant until then.

O November, thou hast caused to cease all growth,
And nature takes a rest from all her work.
The singing birds, the humming bees and butterflies
Cooperate with thee till spring is heard.

I love thee for thine own disarming plots;
How could I say for naught are these bleak days?
How cold the world in death and sorrow gone,
Had I not learned to trust in God always.

*Frost edges maples leaves and creeping Charley in
Manitowoc County, Wisconsin. Photo by Darryl Beers.*

WE SHALL ALL TURN HOMEWARD

Grace Noll Crowell

We shall all turn homeward at the close of day,
Home to lighted windows and a door,
To the warm welcome of a waiting hearth,
To firelight on a floor.

As over marshlands and along strange coasts
The wild fowls beat their swift, unerring way
Back to their reedy nests, so we shall come
Home at the close of day.

Sure of our welcome, confident of rest,
With the same instinct that the wild things know,
We shall turn homeward at the close of day
Through the sunset glow.

And we shall see the casement lamps at last,
Shall pass within to love and warmth and light;
The door will close and shut us safely in
From the fast-gathering night.

Happy the man whose wish and care
A few paternal acres bound,
Content to breathe his native air
In his own ground.
                              —WALTER POPE

A stone wall surrounds a village home in Hillsborough Center,
New Hampshire. Photo by William H. Johnson.

Above left: Identical twins Sydney Claire Borne and Megan Elizabeth Borne are ready to flaunt their fins as they trick-or-treat. These three-year-old mermaids are the granddaughters of Mrs. Don Harris of Thibodaux, Louisiana.

Above center: Heidi Marsh of Seal Beach, California, shares this photo of her daughter, Anneliese, on her first trip to the pumpkin patch. Anneliese stood out as the brightest pumpkin of them all! Heidi tells us that when she was a child, she would fill her red wagon with her art box, canvas, and a copy of *Ideals* for inspiration before walking to art lessons. Now Anneliese is her daily inspiration.

Above right: Mike and Peggy Walters of Boyd, Minnesota, share this photo of their first grandchild, Sarah Elaine Machado. Daughter of Michele and Dan Machado, Sarah Elaine is the "sweet pea" of the family even when out of costume.

Above right: Little Tarin Hanson, daughter of Teresa and Jeff Hanson, announces her choice for this year's favorite pumpkin. This snapshot was sent to us by Tarin's great aunt, Mable Stoltz of Grand Marais, Minnesota.

THANK YOU Mrs. Don Harris, Heidi Marsh, Mike and Peggy Walters, Ruth Giudice, Marie Wachsmuth, Teresa and Jeff Hanson, and Josephine J. Balzer for sharing your family photographs with *Ideals*. We hope to hear from other readers who would like to share snapshots with the *Ideals* family. Please include a self-addressed, stamped envelope if you would like the photos returned. Keep your original photographs for safekeeping and send duplicate photos along with your name, address, and telephone number to:

Readers' Forum
Ideals Publications
535 Metroplex Drive, Suite 250
Nashville, Tennessee 37211

Top left: Autumn is a favorite time of year for three-and-a-half-year-old Ron Coiro, who hopes to someday play quarterback at his favorite college. This snapshot was sent to us by Ron's biggest fan, grandmother Ruth Giudice of Medford, Massachusetts.

Lower left: Marie Wachsmuth of Brentwood, New York, shares this photo of Ringo the beagle, whose curiosity is piqued by the funny-looking orange fellow that is visiting his living room.

Josephine J. Balzer of Prairieville, Louisiana, shares this photo of her grandchildren as they pose happily in the Pilgrim hats they made as a holiday project. Their folded hands and smiling faces are a true indication that they have thankful hearts year-round, not just on Thanksgiving Day. The children are (left to right) Noelle (age two) and Sterling (five), children of Brent and Amy Balzer; and Chaz (three) and Kaeli (five), children of Charles and Carletta Morgan.

ideals

Publisher, Patricia A. Pingry
Editor, Michelle Prater Burke
Designer, Travis Rader
Copy Editor, Amy Johnson
Contributing Editors, Lansing Christman, Pamela Kennedy, Nancy Skarmeas, and Lisa Ragan

ACKNOWLEDGMENTS

CROWELL, GRACE NOLL. "We Shall All Turn Homeward" from *Light of the Years.* Copyright © 1963 by Grace Noll Crowell. Reprinted by arrangement with HarperCollins Publishers. All rights reserved. DRESBACH, GLENN WARD. "On Building a Wood Fire" from *Collected Poems.* Copyright © 1950 by The Caxton Printers, Ltd. Reprinted with permission of the author's estate. FIELD, RUTH B. "Against the Cold." Reprinted with permission of the author's estate. GUEST, EDGAR A. "October." Used by permission of the author's estate. HOLMES, MARJORIE. An excerpt from "Supper's Ready!" from *You and I and Yesterday.* Used by permission of the author. RICHARDSON, ISLA PASCHAL. "Harvest" from *Wind Among the Pines.* Used by permission of Branden Publishing. TIPPETT, JAMES. "Familiar Friends" from *Crickety Cricket! The Best Loved Poems of James S. Tippett.* Copyright © 1933, copyright renewed © 1973 by Martha K. Tippett. Used by permission of HarperCollins Publishers. TREMBLE, STELLA CRAFT. "Thanksgiving." Reprinted with permission of the author's estate. WILSON, CRAIG. "Forever at Home" from USA TODAY, July 28, 1999. Copyright © 1999, USA TODAY. Reprinted with permission. Our sincere thanks to the following authors whom we were unable to locate: Mary Jeannette Bassett for "Woods Path" from *We Ask No Dreams*; Agnes Davenport Bond for "Scarlet Maples" from *Old Rhymes, Old Times*; Anne Campbell for "Apple Butter" from *The Heart of Home*; Kunigunde Duncan for "Fourth Thursday in November" from *Prairie Song*; May Smith White for "Autumn's Glory" and "The Constancy of Seasons"; Esther Wood for "Gray" from *The Wind-Carved Tree.*

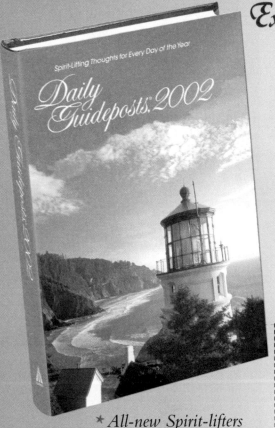

Daily Guideposts 2002
Spirit-Lifting Thoughts for Every Day of the Year

* *All-new Spirit-lifters*
* *New Features*
* *Exciting New Writers*
* *And more*

COMPLETE CARD AND MAIL
TODAY FOR 30-DAYS
FREE EXAMINATION.

Return the reply card today to preview DAILY GUIDEPOSTS, 2002 for 30-days FREE . . . and receive a FREE *Scripture Bookmark*.

Where two or three are gathered together in my name, there am I in the midst of them. —MATTHEW 18:20

FREE SCRIPTURE BOOKMARK included!

NO NEED TO
SEND MONEY NOW!

Explore the wondrous way God stands beside you, prays with you, watches over you each day of your life!

Each of the 365 inspiring devotionals that makes up DAILY GUIDEPOSTS, 2002 is a powerful reminder of God's presence in your life. In them, you'll read the stories of people who have experienced His loving presence in their own lives.

As you share their insights through the year, you'll find yourself growing in faith and you'll learn how to be more aware of the ways God works in your life.

Each selection has been written especially to share the miracle of God's love and the ways He touches our lives. Each devotional speaks to your life and sends you on your way with fresh courage and enthusiasm.

FREE EXAMINATION CERTIFICATE

YES! Rush me DAILY GUIDEPOSTS, 2002 at no risk or obligation , to examine FREE for 30 days. If I decide to keep it, I will be billed at the low Guideposts price of $13.95, plus postage and handling. And if not completely satisfied, I may return the book within 30 days and owe nothing. *As a FREE BONUS with each book, I will receive a Scripture bookmark.*

GIFTS. Send me additional copies as gifts,

Total copies ordered: _____
Regular Print ___ copies (hardcover)   Large Print ___ copies (softcover)
Orders subject to credit approval.
Please print your name and address:

_____
MY NAME
_____
MY ADDRESS
_____
CITY   STATE   ZIP

❑ Please Bill Me ❑ Charge My: ❑ MasterCard   ❑ Visa
Credit Card #:

| | | | | | | | | | | | | | | | |

Expiration Date: _____
Signature _____

Allow 4 weeks for delivery.
Send no money now. We will bill you later.
www.guidepostsbooks.com

Printed in USA
16/201666664

Come home for the holidays . . .
Come back to the sights,
to the sounds, to the spirit of . . .
A Hometown Christmas

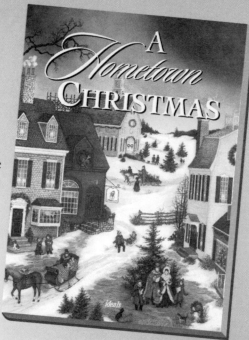

This wonderful book–with it's heartwarming stories, tender poems, and old-fashioned recipes–brings to the reader all of the warmth, togetherness, and love found in the hometowns and in the memories of our hearts at Christmastime.

From the moment you open the front cover, you'll be transported back home through stories about families, neighbors, and friends; through poems that evoke the joy of the season; through songs and recipes that bring back the warm memories; and through photographs and paintings that will remind you of your own hometown.

160 pages, full color throughout, heavy-weight enamel stock, deluxe hardcover binding.

If you long for those Christmases at home . . . if you thrill to the sound of sleighbells and carols . . . if you love the true Spirit of Christmas . . . you owe it to yourself to take advantage of our offer of a free look at this outstanding collection of the warmth and wonder of Christmas.

Return the reply card today to preview *A HOMETOWN CHRISTMAS* for 30-days FREE . . . and receive a FREE set of Christmas Scenic Postcards.